SCHOLASTIC

Essential English

Course Book

Level 2

Page 108 constitutes an extension of the copyright page.

Published by Scholastic India Pvt. Ltd.
A subsidiary of Scholastic Inc., New York, 10012 (USA).
Publishers since 1920, with international operations in Canada, Australia, New Zealand, the United Kingdom, Mexico, India, Argentina, and Hong Kong.

For information regarding permission, write to:
Scholastic India Pvt. Ltd.
A-27, Ground Floor, Bharti Sigma Centre
Infocity-1, Sector 34, Gurgaon (Haryana) - 122001
Email: info_in@scholastic.asia

Typeset at Digital Expressions

First edition: 2008
Reprinted: 2009 (twice), 2010 (twice), 2011, 2012, 2013, 2014 (twice), 2016, 2024, 2026

ISBN: 978-81-8477-140-4

Printed at : Saurabh Printers Pvt. Ltd.

Contents

			Language Development		
	Lesson	**Reading Comprehension**	**Vocabulary**	**Grammar**	**Spelling & Punctuation**
1	Jay and the Baby (Rebus)				
2	His Majesty's Moustache (Story)	Match the columns	Naming the months of the year/Naming everyday objects	Common nouns and proper nouns/Singular and plural nouns	Using capital letters and full stops
3	Springtime on the Farm (Play)	Questions and answers	Naming animal babies/Unscrambling words	Common nouns and proper nouns/Making a sentence	Using capital letters
4	A Dinosaur was at My Door (Poem)	Questions and answers/Finding words in a grid	Comparisons/Silent letters	Adjectives/Articles	Reading and spelling 'sh', 'ch' and 'th' words
5	The Emperor and the Nightingale (Story)	Questions and answers/True or false	Naming furniture	Masculine and feminine nouns/Common nouns	Reading and spelling double consonant words
6	Eyes to See (Poem)	Questions and answers	Words about feelings/Rhyming words	Adverbs/Nouns and adjectives	Naming doers
7	The Sun God (Non-fiction: world myths)	Questions and answers	Professions	Adding 'ing' to verbs/Has, had or have	Reading and spelling 'ie' words
8	In the Desert (Non-fiction: geography)	Questions and answers	Identifying odd words/Words describing the weather	Past tense/Adjectives	Using question marks/ Reading and spelling 'kn' words
9	The Owl and the Pussycat (Poem)	Questions and answers	Describing yourself		
10.	Helen Keller (Biography)	Questions and answers	Opposites	Nouns and verbs	Reading and spelling words ending with 'ss' and 'sh'
11	Tiny Turtle Wants a Friend (Story)	Questions and answers	Animal sounds	Sentences/Helping verbs	Reading and spelling 'ea' words
12	Four Little Tigers (Poem)	Questions and answers	Rhyming words/Identifying endangered animals/ Identifying kitchen items	Pronouns	Reading and spelling 'cl', 'fl' and 'pl' words/ Punctuation marks
13	Sir No-name (Story)	Questions and answers	Naming vehicles/Words that go together	Using 'there is/was/are/were'/ Question words	Reading and spelling words ending with 'er' and 'or'
14	How the Leopard Got its Spots (Story)	Questions and answers	Synonyms/Naming clothes	Prepositions	Reading and spelling 'ck' and 'sw' words
15	I'm a Real Boy (Poem)	True or false	Comparisons	Joining words/Identifying parts of speech	Reading and spelling 'br', 'dr', 'fr' and 'tr' words

Communication Skills			Social Skills	Fun Time
Writing	**Listening**	**Speaking**	**Everyday English**	**Activity**
				Safe or unsafe?
Completing sentences	Listening for nouns	Asking and answering questions		Join the dots
Fill in the blanks	Listening to identify	Discussing animals		Little words from big words
			At a resturaunt	Naming seasonal vegetables
Completing sentences	Listening to draw	Asking for permission		Crossword
		Meeting a friend		Writing a poem
Writing about holidays	Listening to write	Talking about preferences	Making requests	Colouring
Asking questions	Listening to repeat	Making suggestions		Desert objects
	Listening for adjectives	Discussing holiday plans		Nursery rhymes
Sequencing a story	Following instructions	Talking about preferences		Make a bookworm
Picture composition	Listening for doing words	Talking about your friend		Pet puzzler
Sentences on a given subject	Listening for missing words	Talking while doing something	Asking for permission	
Describing your home	Listening for colours	Discussing your hobbies		Crossword
Describing a picture	Listening for odd words	Discussing food		Colouring from a given description
	Listening for homonyms	Class discussion	Apologising	Same or different?

* Listening activity texts are provided at the end of the book.

Thank You!

The *Essential English* books were sent out to approximately eighty schools across the country for primary school principals, departmental heads and teachers to give their feedback on the contents.

The publishers would like to thank all those who took the time out of their busy schedules to go through the books and make many valuable suggestions, which have been duly incorporated.

Abha Arora, Delhi Public School, Chandigarh
Alka Patankar, Sanskriti School, New Delhi
Angela Ghosh, St James' School, Kolkata
Anjali, Yadavindra Public School, Patiala
Anjum Rahim, Delhi Public School, Raipur
Arpita Anand, Navy Children's School, New Delhi
Ch. Naveena Kumari, BSD DAV Public School, Hyderabad
Chandana, Lancer's Convent, New Delhi
Garima Wadhwa, Bal Bharati Public School, New Delhi
Harmeen Kaur, Delhi Public School, Chandigarh
Harmeet Kaur, St Mark's Senior Secondary Public School, New Delhi
Intu Ghuman, Yadavindra Public School, Patiala
Iyer Rama Chandrashekar, Sunshine School, Rajkot
Kanika Kumar, Lancer's Convent, New Delhi
Lakshmi Satish, Head Start Learning Centre, Chennai
Lakshmi Subramanian, consultant, Hyderabad
Maneesha Gupta, Sanskriti School, New Delhi
Manju Gupta, Pallavi Model School, Hyderabad
Matthew Panamkat, Doon Public School, New Delhi
Mitali Ghosh, Sunshine School, Rajkot
Monica Keswani, Bal Bharati Public School, New Delhi
N. Purohit, Sunshine School, Rajkot
N.R. Sailaja, BSD DAV Public School, Hyderabad
Nandita Majumdar, BSD DAV Public School, Hyderabad
Neeru Bhaskar, Delhi Public School, Kanpur
Nirmal Muku, Vidya Niketan Senior Secondary School, New Delhi
Padma Singh, Pallavi Model School, Hyderabad
Pamela Banerjee, Delhi Public School, Kanpur
Peter Lauenstein Denzongpa, Taktse International School, Sikkim
Pooja Khurana, Lancer's Convent, New Delhi
Priti Kathpalia, Sanskriti School, New Delhi
Priyanka Khare, Delhi Public School, Raipur
Priyanka, Lancer's Convent, New Delhi
R. Sumathy, Delhi Public School, Raipur
Ravneet Walia, Yadavindra Public School, Patiala
Reena Nagpal, Yadavindra Public School, Patiala
Renu Vashishta, Maharana Mewar Vidya Mandir, Udaipur
Renuka, Lancer's Convent, New Delhi
Reshma Thapa, Taktse International School, Sikkim
Rima Nijh, Delhi Public School, Chandigarh
Rinku Bhowmick, Navy Children's School, New Delhi
Ritika Sharma, Navy Children's School, New Delhi
Roma Gupta, Navy Children's School, New Delhi
Rubina Majid, school consultant, Hyderabad
Ruchi Verma, Delhi Public School, Chandigarh
S. Purushutham, Delhi Public School, Raipur
S. Sivasankari, Delhi Public School, Raipur
S.K. Sodhi, BSD DAV Public School, Hyderabad
Sabira A. Dal, Sunshine School, Rajkot
Sangeeta Chaudhury, The Gurukul, Panchkula
Sangeeta Sharma, Delhi Public School, Chandigarh
Sangita Malik, Yadavindra Public School, Patiala
Sarika Kapoor, Lancer's Convent, New Delhi
Sarita, Lancer's Convent, New Delhi
Savithri Radhakrishnan, Head Start Learning Centre, Chennai
Seema Pathak, Vidya Niketan, New Delhi
Sharon Galstaun, St Karen's Nursery School, Patna
Shylaja R., AMM Matriculation Higher Secondary School, Chennai
Sister Philomena, Holy Cross English Primary School, Aurangabad
Sonia Dheer, The Gurukul, Panchkula
Sonisha, Lancer's Convent, New Delhi
Sudha Suresh, Vidya Mandir Senior Secondary School, Chennai
Suman Lata Pradhan, Taktse International School, Sikkim
T. Sharada, Lancer's Convent, New Delhi
T.S.S. Reddy, consultant, Hyderabad
Teena Agarwal, Bal Bharati Public School, New Delhi
The teachers of G.D. Goenka Public School, New Delhi
The teachers of St Mark's Senior Secondary Public School, New Delhi
V. Subhashini, Subhaniketan, Kakinada
Vaishali and Manisha Gadekar, Kids Edutainment Centre, Mumbai
Varnika, Lancer's Convent, New Delhi
Veena S. Kumar, Navy Children's School, New Delhi
Vishali Kapoor, Delhi Public School, Kanpur
Y. Cabral, Methodist High School, Kanpur

In addition to the people listed above, there were many teachers who did not want their help to be publicly acknowledged. In deference to their wishes, we have not included their names, but we would once again like to acknowledge their valuable help.

Introduction

Essential English, a series of innovative activity-based course books, is a valuable learning tool. The books use the communicative approach to help students improve their written and verbal skills and appreciate how the various elements of English are used to convey meaning. The approach follows the current NCERT curriculum and pedagogical principles.

In addition, the books aim to foster a love of literature and reading in children. This has been done by a careful selection of age-appropriate literary pieces by well-known Indian and international authors, designed to stimulate children's imagination and inculcate a life-long interest in reading.

The books have been created by a panel of eminent authors, school and college teachers, and experienced children's publishers, and vetted by school teachers and principals from different parts of India.

The *Essential English* series has been designed to cover the essential skills of the language:

Language development:

- Reading comprehension
- Vocabulary
- Grammar
- Spelling and punctuation

Communication skills:

- Writing
- Listening
- Speaking

Social and other skills:

- Everyday English
- Activity
- Read More (for Classes IV and V)

Some of the unique features of this series are:

The selection of texts

You will notice from the table of contents that the books contain an interesting mix of short stories by distinguished authors, extracts from well-known novels, poems, plays, speeches, biographies and non-fiction articles on varied subjects. The texts selected are both classic and contemporary so that students are introduced to different kinds of writing. Students will enjoy reading a wide variety of stories and articles that are humorous, exciting and informative.

Introduction to well-loved authors

The authors for most of the pieces are well-known Indian or international authors, who write for the appropriate age group. We believe that reading the finest writing available in a range of different styles will aid children to learn the language better.

Illustrations in diverse styles

Each text is illustrated in a style appropriate to its contents with paintings, pencil sketches, collages or photographs to encourage the child's aesthetic appreciation of different kinds of art.

Encouragement to understand and analyse

The reading comprehension sections are a combination of inference questions designed to make the child read the text closely, and critical response questions that encourage the child to think and analyse character, situation, moral values and ideas. The poems are followed by questions to make the child appreciate poetry and understand the different nuances of the poem.

Learning through fun

The activities include word puzzles, riddles and other fun ways of finding answers and are tools for improving comprehension. Finding the main idea, paying attention to details, drawing conclusions and following directions are just some of the skills included.

Learning through practice

Each lesson contains challenging vocabulary and grammar sections. The grammar exercises are contextualised to contribute meaningfully to children's written and verbal abilities.

Reinforcing concepts

A recap of grammar and vocabulary concepts and terms ensures that old lessons are reinforced at every level and the child's recollection of concepts is refreshed before he or she embarks on new and more challenging exercises.

Speaking and listening exercises

These sections are designed to help students communicate in English with correct pronunciation. The exercises help the child to learn to speak with confidence and to listen carefully. The speaking sections give the child practice in diverse kinds of speaking, such as interviews, class discussions, describing, giving directions, and sharing information. The listening exercises teach a child to respond to various oral problems.

Writing exercises

Essential English has sections that will help students develop independent writing skills. Level-appropriate activities—such as writing stories, letters and paragraphs, book reviews, diary entries, invitation cards, thank-you notes—stimulate and encourage students to plan, expand and proofread their work.

Everyday English

This is a unique forum where students can apply the language to interact in day-to-day activities. Simple exercises, such as ordering food, giving directions and asking the time, help students to confidently speak in English, and learn the vocabulary and expressions appropriate for common life experiences.

Fun-filled activities

These learner-centred sections introduce children to entertaining and creative craft projects, crosswords, word games, logic and reasoning games, cracking codes and so on. Although presented as games, these exercises are a vital part of the learning process and help children learn essential language skills.

Encouragement to read more

Essential English 4 and *5* include a Read More section, which provides information about the author and the extract/story. It introduces children to more books by the same author or to other books in the same genre. This is to motivate children to find appropriate reading material that fits in with their interests from the school library.

Acquiring tools for independent learning

The children are taught to use the dictionary and thesaurus, to do basic research individually or in groups, and to present reports, all of which are independent learning skills crucial for middle and senior school.

With an understanding of the age-appropriate rules and elements that govern English, *Essential English* will help students to communicate correctly and effectively.

Jay and the Baby 1

Can you read this picture story by Sumathi Sudhakar?

Jay was happy. Mummy would bring home a  soon.

"Is it a boy or a girl?"  asked Daddy as he took  to the .

"Wait and see,"  laughed.

All morning, Jay stood near the . "Is it a girl or a boy?" he asked Grandma. "I don't know," said . "But you had better get your room ready for the baby."

 ran to his room. He put a  in the baby's . Then he put away his  neatly. Now there was room for the baby's

toys too. He also cleaned his  and made space for the

baby's  .

He put the big  near the cradle. "For baby!" he said.

Just then the  rang. It was Daddy! "Your sister is

coming home, Jay!" he said. "Get ready to welcome her!"

"Yay!"  shouted in joy.

 thought his sister looked funny. She had very little hair on her .

She had no teeth in her . Her  were very small and almost

always closed. Her 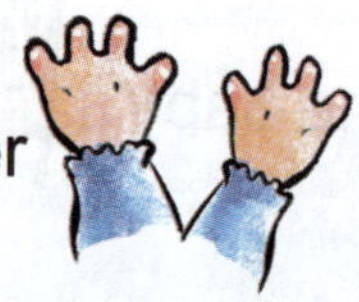 and 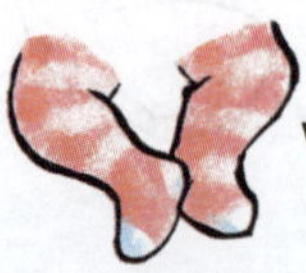 were tiny and round.

She did not know anything. She could not speak. She cried when she was hungry. Then Mummy would give her milk in a feeding  .

Sometimes the milk dripped out from her  . So Mummy

tied a  around her neck so she would not mess her

 . She slept all day in her  .

If you switched off the fan, she woke up and cried. She loved

to watch the  turn round and round.

When the baby was happy, she smiled, waved her 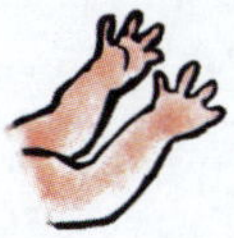 and her  .

Activity

Safe or unsafe?

Circle the things that are safe for the baby to play with.

His Majesty's Moustache 2

You must have heard of Akbar and Birbal. This is a funny story about the famous emperor and clever Birbal, based on a story by Anupa Lal.

One evening, King Akbar said to his noblemen, "Tell me, what should be the punishment for someone who dared to pinch my moustache?"

The men were shocked. Then Shahbaz Khan spoke up. "He should be whipped."

"His head should be cut off, Your Honour!" said Mulla Do Piaza.

"The person should be hanged!" said Shadi Shah.

"And you, Birbal? What do you suggest?" asked Akbar.

"I would give him some sweets," said Birbal calmly.

Everyone present was surprised. Had Birbal gone mad? Sweets for such an act?

Akbar frowned. "Did I hear you right, Birbal?" he said. "You consider sweets a suitable punishment?"

"Only in your case, Your Majesty," said Birbal. "Who else but your grandson would dare to touch your moustache?"

Akbar burst out laughing. "It was indeed the little grandson!" he said. "And I did give him sweets, too. Birbal, as usual, you are right!"

Reading Comprehension

The following punishments were suggested by Akbar's noblemen. Match the names of the men to the punishment they suggested.

Shadi Shah	head should be cut off
Shahbaz Khan	given sweets
Mulla Do Piaza	should be whipped
Birbal	should be hanged

Vocabulary

This is a list of the months of the year. But some are missing! Complete the list by filling the names of the months that have been left out.

January	May	September
February	____________	____________
March	July	____________
____________	August	December

Find the names of the following objects in the grid.

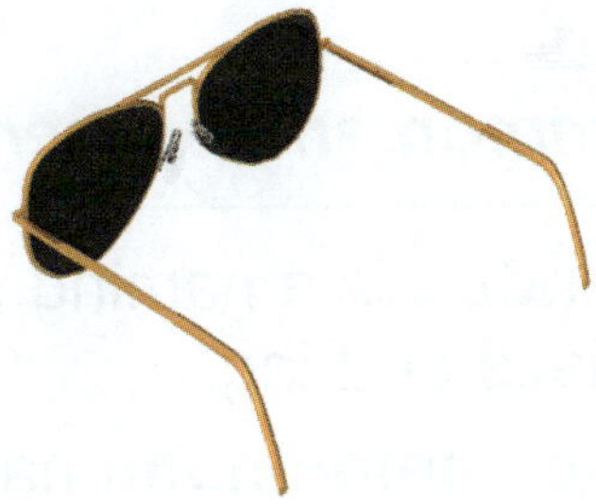

T	E	L	E	P	H	O	N	E
A	P	P	E	H	O	T	E	A
B	O	O	K	I	D	J	W	J
O	G	L	A	S	S	E	S	U
W	Q	C	V	Y	B	N	P	K
K	W	H	A	N	D	B	A	G
E	E	F	R	C	E	D	P	Z
Y	G	P	E	N	S	G	E	L
S	X	M	I	R	R	O	R	M

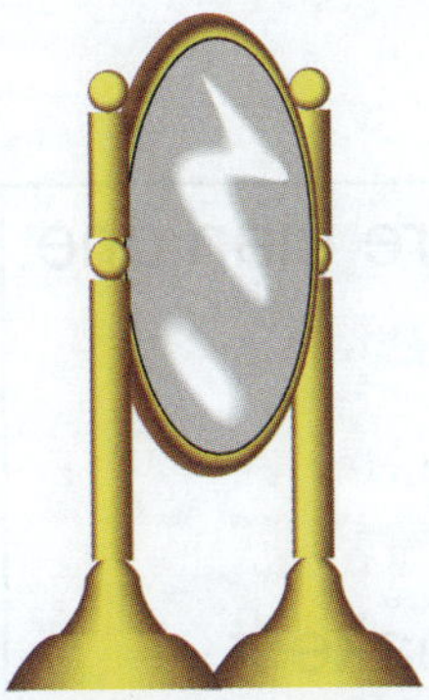

Grammar

Common and proper nouns

A **noun** is a naming word. It is a word that names a person, animal, place or thing.

A **common noun** names any regular, ordinary person, animal, place or thing. For example: bus, boy, city.

A **proper noun** names a very specific, particular person, animal, place or thing. For example: Agra, Rahul, Himalaya.

Classify the following nouns as common and proper.

Abhinav doll car table Bangalore Egypt man Almas

Common Nouns	Proper Nouns

Singular and plural nouns

Singular means one of something. **Plural** means more than one. Some rules:

- You can make most nouns plural by just adding -s.
  For example: pencil: pencils.
- If the noun ends with s, ch, sh, x or z, add -es to make it plural.
  For example: fox: foxes, church: churches.
- Drop the y and add -ies if the letter in front of the y is a consonant. For example: berry: berries.

Change the following words from singular to plural by adding -s, -es or -ies.

apple ______________________

boat ______________________

match ______________________

tiger ______________________

tub ______________________

cherry ______________________

pony ______________________

bush ______________________

baby ______________________

bus ______________________

chair ______________________

taxi ______________________

Spelling and Punctuation

Capital letters are used for:

- the first word in a sentence.
- proper nouns.
- the first spoken word in a dialogue.

Full stops are used at the end of statements and commands.

Rewrite the following sentences using capital letters and full stops.

1. king akbar was in the courtyard talking to his courtiers
2. the courtiers felt that the offender should be punished
3. everyone was amazed by what birbal said
4. akbar told birbal "as usual you are right"
5. akbar gave his grandson sweets

Writing

Fill in the blanks.

Shahbaz Khan thought that the offender should be ____________ .

Birbal thought that he should be given ______________.

King Akbar's ______________ had dared to pinch his moustache.

King Akbar had actually given ______________ to his grandson.

Listening

Your teacher will read a passage. As he/she reads, write the nouns that you hear in the passage.

Speaking

Take turns with your partner to ask questions and answer them.

Here are some of the questions you could ask each other:

- What is your favourite colour?
- Which subject do you like?
- Who is your best friend?

Activity

Join the dots

Join the dots to discover the picture, and colour the picture.

3 Springtime on the Farm

This short play by Carol Pugliano-Martin describes the miracle of new life.

Characters

FARMER	SHEEP	COW	DUCK
HEN	LAMB	KITTENS	DUCKLINGS
CHICKS	CAT	CALF	PIGLETS

FARMER: I am so excited! Spring is really great. So much is going to happen. I can hardly wait!

HEN: After sitting on my eggs, I just hatched some chicks.

CHICKS: Now we're snug and cosy in our nest of straw and sticks.

SHEEP: Come and meet my little lamb. He is almost fast asleep.

LAMB: When I grow up I want to be the biggest woolly sheep.

CAT: I just had some kittens.

COW: And I just had a calf.

KITTENS AND CALF: And when we play together, everyone has a laugh.

DUCK: Look at my ducklings.

DUCKLINGS: All we do is quack.

PIGLETS: We piglets cannot wait until our next yummy snack!

FARMER: It's great to be a farmer, especially in spring. Meeting lots of brand-new friends is such a special thing!

Read the play aloud in class with students reading the parts of the different characters.

Reading Comprehension

Answer the following questions.

1. Why is the farmer so excited?
2. What is the chicks' nest made of?
3. What does the lamb want to be when it grows up?
4. What do the ducklings do?
5. Why does the farmer meet new friends in spring?

Vocabulary

In the play there are lots of animals and their babies.

Fill the table below with the names of animals and their babies.

Animal	Baby
hen	
	piglet
	foal
duck	
	lamb
cat	
	puppy
cow	

Unscramble the following words to get the names of some animals you can find on a farm.

LUBL ________	PHESE ________	BLAM ________	GPI ________
CUKD ________	HROES ________	KIHCC ________	FLAC ________

Grammar

Underline the common nouns in **green** and the proper nouns in **red** in the following sentences.

Pushpa and Raman are in class.

This is my friend Neha.

My mother and father went to Ladakh.

My cousins from Chennai are here.

We can take a plane or a train to Delhi.

Kamini and Kalyani are sisters.

Making a sentence

A sentence is a group of words that expresses a thought.

Unscramble these sets of words to make sentences.

Don't forget to start the first word with a capital letter and end the sentence with a full stop.

1. table the book on is the
2. drink we milk at all night
3. bed o'clock go I to ten at
4. want to they football play
5. sister dance my nidhi classes to goes

Spelling and Punctuation

Correct the sentences by using capital letters in the correct places.

1. last week i watched a movie with ria and ramya.
2. my friend himani comes from chandigarh.
3. please help pooja collect her books.
4. that pencil belongs to angad.
5. we are going to italy, france and germany.
6. that is my brother rishabh.

Writing

Fill in the blanks.

The farmer is ____________ about spring.

The hen sat on her _________ to ________ some chicks.

The chicks in their nest feel ________ and ___________.

Sheep and lambs are covered in ____________.

The __________ only quack.

The ______________ likes meeting new ___________ in spring.

Listening

Your teacher will read out some clues. Listen carefully and guess the animal that he/she is talking about.

Speaking

Do you like animals? Discuss with your partner which animals you like, which ones you don't like, and which animals you are scared of.

Give reasons. Are your reasons the same as your partner's?

- I like dogs because they are friendly.
- I am scared of cats because they have sharp claws.

Activity

Little words from big words

Find a little word in each of the big words and write it on the line below. Then draw pictures of what you have found.

elephant	then	beggar	card
 *ant*			
crater	pansy	brain	fowl

4 A Dinosaur Was at My Door

What happens when a dinosaur comes for lunch? Find out in this poem by Mary Sullivan.

A dinosaur was at my door.
He said he'd come for lunch.

And so I said, "Do come right in—
I've some veggies you can munch!"

He ate cabbage and corn
And tomatoes and beans.

And spinach and lettuce
And lots of fresh greens.

He had cauliflower, beetroots,
Brinjal and such.

He ate turnips and capsicum
And chillies (not too much)!

He ate onions, cucumber,
Peas and tomatoes.

Pumpkin, carrots,
Mushrooms, potatoes ...

"Aren't you almost full?"
I asked him politely.

"I've saved room for dessert,"
He answered me brightly!

Reading Comprehension

Answer the following questions.

1. Why did the dinosaur come to the poet's house?
2. What did the poet offer the dinosaur?
3. What did the dinosaur save room for?

The names of some vegetables that the dinosaur ate are hidden in the word grid.

Find the names of the following vegetables.

carrots peas potatoes tomatoes cabbage corn

B	V	C	A	B	B	A	G	E
T	O	M	A	T	O	E	S	L
H	Y	D	M	T	P	O	E	U
S	C	A	R	R	O	T	S	P
W	O	C	N	G	L	O	T	E
T	R	S	V	J	K	J	V	A
U	N	U	N	G	J	H	M	S
P	O	T	A	T	O	E	S	W
I	M	O	Q	S	P	E	K	D

Vocabulary

We often use comparisons in which we describe something by comparing it to something else. For example: As cold as ice. As dry as dust.

Choose the correct word from the brackets to complete the following comparisons.

As cold as ____________ (ice/fire)

As hard as ____________ (wool/stone)

As good as ____________ (new/old)

As white as ____________ (snow/coal)

As black as ____________ (day/night)

As smooth as ____________ (sand/glass)

As high as a ____________ (kite/bicycle)

When we say the word knife, the letter k is not pronounced. It is a **silent letter**.

Read the following words and underline the silent letter in all of them.

calf	talk	edge	Wednesday
honest	half	sign	badge
walk	palm	tongue	guest
listen	autumn	biscuit	knife

Grammar

Adjectives

An **adjective** is a word that describes or tells us more about the noun. For example: the blue shirt, the kind man, the tall building. Some describing words, such as one cat or three pillows, are numbers. But there are other number words that can be used to describe things—some, many, few, much and most.

Choose the correct words to complete the following sentences.

_________ students in the class are very good. (much/most)

________ children travel to school by car. (much/few)

You have eaten too ________ sweets. (many/some)

When people eat too __________ they become ill. (much/some)

Would you like _____________ juice? (some/few)

I have ________ friends because I am a new student. (much/few)

Articles

A, an and the are the three articles. They are noun signals and tell you that there is a noun coming up in the sentence.

- The is used for a specific thing. For example: the big book, the king of Arabia.
- A and an are used for any one of a group of things. For example: an orange, a hat.
- An is used instead of a in front of words that begin with a vowel (a, e, i, o, u). An is also used in front of words that begin with a silent h.

Fill in the blanks with a, an or the.

Your breakfast is on ________ table.

At the zoo I saw ______ giraffe, ______ tiger and ______ elephant.

Amira gave the teacher _______ apple.

There are twenty students in _________ class.

________ new student is very tall.

There is ______ banyan tree in front of the house.

Spelling and Punctuation

The following words contain ch, sh and th. Read them aloud.

shore
she
shape
a**sh**
shell

show
there
thin
thank
ma**th**s

dea**th**
wea**th**er
chip
chur**ch**
chin

child
cheek
chap

Fill in the blanks with th, ch or sh to complete the following words.
The clues given in the brackets will help you.

__ __ air (something we sit on)

__ __ eep (a farm animal)

__ __ ocolate (something that is very good to eat)

pa __ __ (a place to walk)

__ __ip (a way to travel across the sea)

tea __ __ er (someone we see in school)

mo __ __ er (a member of your family)

__ __ row (the opposite of catch)

__ __ ark (dangerous sea animal)

__ __ op (where you go to buy things)

Everyday English

Pretend that you are in a restaurant. Take turns with your partner to be the waiter and the customer.

You could use some of the phrases in the box.

- May I have a glass of water, please?
- Please bring me the menu
- Will you have dessert?
- Can I have the bill, please?

Activity

Find out the names of three summer vegetables and three winter vegetables.

5 The Emperor and the Nightingale

This is one of the most famous stories by Hans Christian Andersen.

Many years ago in China, there lived a nightingale. One day, the Chinese emperor heard about a nightingale who sang beautifully. He said to one of his noblemen, "Find this wonderful bird for me."

The nobleman went through the whole palace but no one had heard of the bird. Finally, he met a poor little girl in the kitchen, who said, "Oh, yes, I know the nightingale. Every evening, I sit in the woods and listen to its song."

"Take us to the nightingale," said the nobleman. So she went into the woods, and half the court followed her. The nightingale began to sing.

"There she is," said the girl, pointing to a little brown bird sitting on a branch.

"Little nightingale, please come to the court this evening," said the nobleman.

"It will be my pleasure," said the bird.

That night the nightingale sang so sweetly that tears came into the emperor's eyes. The emperor liked the nightingale so much that he asked her to remain at court and live in a cage.

One day, someone gifted the emperor an artificial nightingale covered with diamonds, and rubies. As soon as it was wound up, it sang and moved its tail up and down.

Everyone loved hearing the artificial bird sing. No one noticed that the living nightingale had flown back to her own green woods.

The artificial bird sang every day. One evening, when it was singing, something inside the bird cracked, and the music stopped. And nobody could fix it.

The emperor fell ill. He lay in his bed and shouted, "Sing, golden bird! Sing!" But the bird was silent.

Suddenly the sound of sweet music came through the window. Outside, on a tree, sat the living nightingale. And as she sang, the emperor started getting better.

"Thank you, little bird. I know you well. I forgot you, and yet you have saved me with your sweet song. You must stay with me," said the emperor.

"No," replied the nightingale. "I cannot live in the palace, but let me come when I like. I will sing to you, so that you may be happy." So saying, she flew away.

Reading Comprehension

Answer the following questions.

1. Where did the nightingale live?
2. What task did the Chinese emperor give the nobleman?
3. Who took the nobleman to the nightingale?
4. What was the artificial nightingale covered with?
5. Why did the artificial bird stop singing?

Mark true (T) or false (F).

The living nightingale sang very well. ☐

Everyone in the palace had heard about the nightingale. ☐

The emperor liked the nightingale's song. ☐

The artificial nightingale could not be fixed. ☐

The living nightingale lived in a cage in the palace. ☐

Vocabulary

These objects are pieces of furniture you might find in a house.
Write their names next to the pictures.

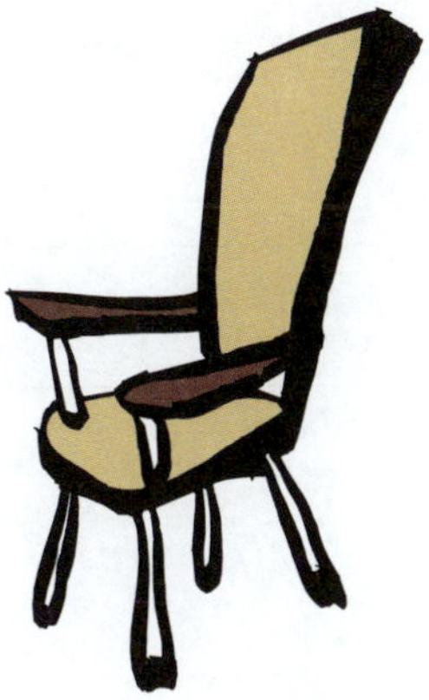

Make a list of all the furniture that you can think of from your house. Ask your teacher for help.

Grammar

Masculine and feminine nouns

Living beings can have different names depending on whether they are male (masculine) or female (feminine). Many common nouns, such as engineer or teacher, can refer to both men and women.

Write the masculine form of the following words.

mother ____________ woman ____________

queen ____________ hen ____________

cow ____________

Write the feminine form of the following words.

brother ____________ son ____________

emperor ____________ grandfather ____________

boy ____________

Underline the words that refer to both male and female.

student	baby	teacher	artist
doctor	mother	nephew	princess
father	parent	writer	

Spelling and Punctuation

What do you notice about the following words?

pu**ll** ha**pp**y ha**mm**er spa**rr**ow ho**pp**ing wa**gg**ing ra**bb**it

Choose letters from the box to complete these words:

rr bb pp ll tt mm

pu ___ ___ y hu ___ ___ ing bu ___ ___ le su ___ ___ er

ki ___ ___ en fa ___ ___ ing a ___ ___ le ca ___ ___ ot

a ___ ___ ow ba ___ ___ le bu ___ ___

Writing

Complete the following sentences.

The little girl led half the court into the ______________________________.

When the artificial bird was wound up, it ____________________________.

The nightingale flew back
to the woods when ____.

The emperor heard sweet music coming __________________________.

The emperor got better when ____________________________________.

Listening

Listen to the instructions read out by your teacher. Draw what you hear.

Speaking

Practice asking for permission with your partner.

You could use the following.

- May I borrow your pencil?
- Sorry, I am using it.
- May I look at your picture?
- Yes, of course.

Activity

Crossword

Can you complete this crossword with the names of birds?

ACROSS

2 it clucks

4 it quacks

5 night bird

DOWN

1 small brown bird

6 large black bird with loud caw

3 it sang to the emperor

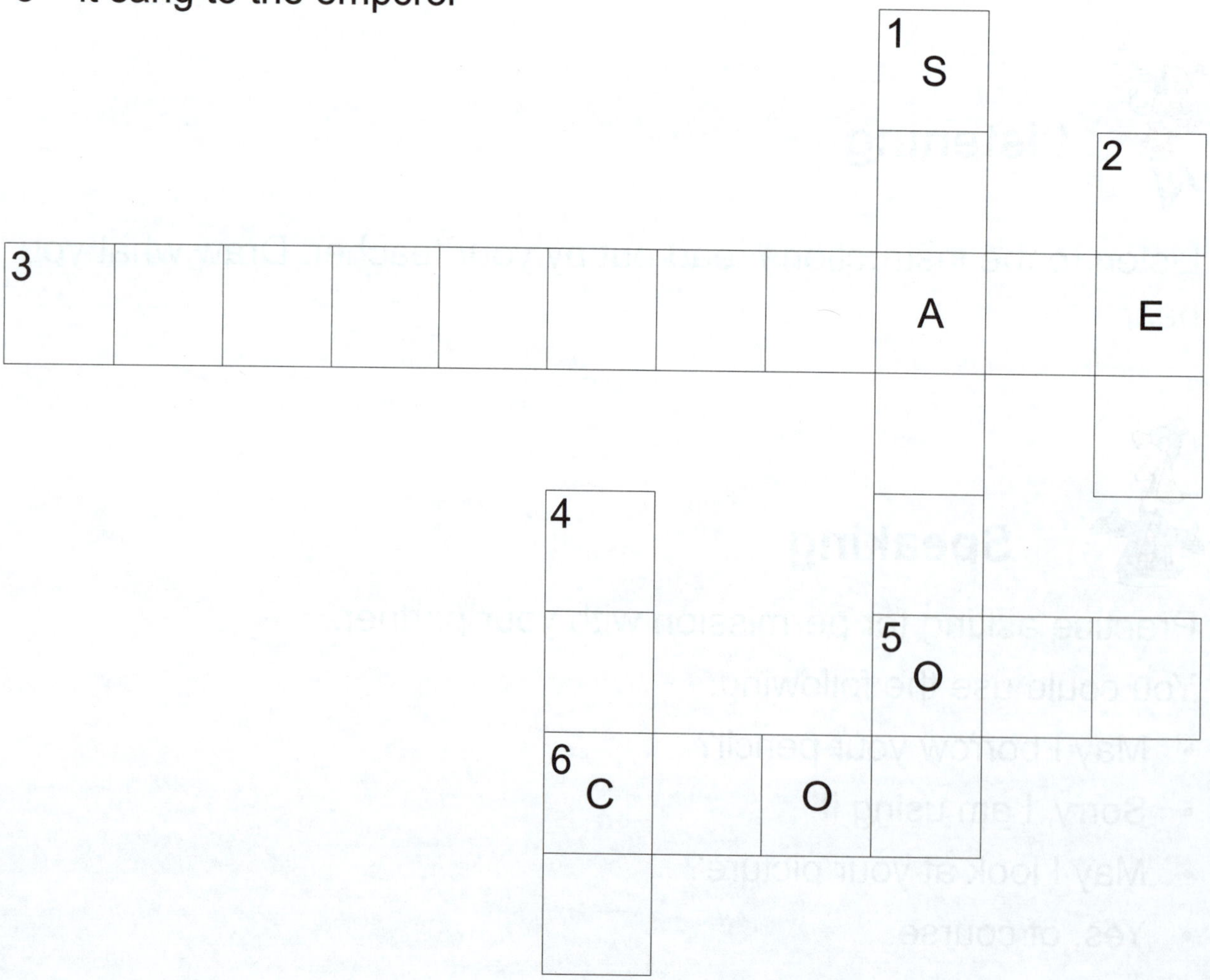

Eyes to See 6

This poem by Mary Sullivan talks about how special our powers are.

What luck that we have eyes to see,
The morning light,
The stars at night,
The blueness of the sea.

What luck that we have eyes to see,
The gentle deer,
Her fawn so near,
All creatures wild and free.

What luck that we have eyes to see,
The clouds floating on a breeze,
Happy green swaying trees,
A field of flowers lovely as can be!

What luck that we have eyes to see,
The sun above,
The ones we love,
How lucky can we be!

Reading Comprehension

Answer the following questions.

1. What is the colour of the sea?
2. What are the things that you see in the sky?
3. What is a fawn?
4. What words does the poet use to describe the trees?

Vocabulary

The poet feels happy and lucky to be able to see the wonderful things in the world around him. The words in the box all describe people's feelings.

Complete the sentences below by choosing words from the box.

happy sad lonely scared angry excited bored worried

I am very _______________ when my friends are away.

Travelling on an airplane makes me feel _______________.

Sometimes the students are _______________ during classes.

My sister is __________ about her exam results.

Seeing my grandparents makes me _______________.

During the movie I felt _______________.

When people say rude things I become _______________.

In the poem, see and sea, and night and light are sets of rhyming words.

What are the other rhyming words in the poem?

Find words that rhyme with the words given below.

bake: lake, make, ____________________

bed: head, said, ____________________

tree: free, ____________________

bear: ____________________

man: ____________________

eye: ____________________

green: ____________________

bell: ____________________

Grammar

We sometimes use words ending in -ly to describe an action. For example, in the sentence Nina walked quickly towards the shop, quickly describes the way Nina walked. Usually these words are made by adding -ly to a describing word.

Complete the following sentences with words that describe the actions. Use the words in brackets to help you.

The koel sang ____________. (sweet)

After completing their work, the children talked ____________. (soft)

"Go away!" the old lion roared ____________. (loud)

You should do your homework ______________ and ______________. (neat, careful)

Wait ____________ until the doctor is free. (patient)

The candles are burning ______________. (bright)

Underline the naming words (nouns) in **blue** and describing words (adjectives) in **red**.

The big grey horse drank water from the stream.

The hungry children were hoping for a hot meal.

Candice and Abhay smelled the red and yellow flowers in the beautiful garden.

I am shivering because this room is very cold.

This brown chair is the most comfortable one in the room.

Spelling and Punctuation

We make the names of people who are doing an action by adding -er or -r to the doing word. Someone who bakes is a baker. Someone who plays cricket is a cricketer, or a cricket player.

Fill in the blanks.

I dance. I am a ____________.

I play football. I am a ________________.

I photograph beautiful things. I am a _________________.

I teach children. I am a ____________________.

I sing songs. I am a ________________.

I write stories. I am a ________________.

Speaking

Pretend that you are meeting your friend during the holidays. Have a conversation with your partner.

You can use some of the words and phrases in the box.

hello goodbye how are you family journey fun play please

Activity

Write a poem about your nose.

7 The Sun God

This informative piece about the sun god is taken from The Cowherd Prince and Other Gods and Goddesses *by Sheila Dhir.*

In India, the sun god is known as Surya. Since the day is measured by the rising and setting of the sun, Surya is considered the time-keeper of the world.

Surya was very bright and very hot. Surya's wife Sanjana could not bear the light and heat, and decided to run away. She turned into a mare and hid in the forest. Surya turned into a horse and found her. She returned to him and they lived happily together. But because Surya was so bright and hot, Sanjana was always tired. Her father then made Surya's heat less so that Sanjana could live easily with her husband.

In ancient Egypt, the sun god was known as Re. He was also believed to be the creator of the world. At the start of time, an egg came out of the water and Re climbed out of its shell. He then had two children who became the atmosphere and clouds. They in turn had more children, Geb and Nut, who became the earth and the stars. One day, Re started crying and humans were made from his tears. He also created the four seasons.

In old Japan, Amaterasu was the sun goddess. When her brother Susanowo treated her badly, she hid in heaven's cave and blocked the entrance with a huge stone. The world became dark, and evil spirits came out of their hiding places. The gods then held a meeting and decided to trick Amaterasu into coming out by having a party near the cave. They put a big mirror in front of the cave and beautiful jewels on a tree. Then they began dancing to loud music. Amaterasu heard the music and laughter, and took a look outside. She loved her own brilliant reflection in the mirror so much that she came out of the cave. Finally, the light covered and coloured the world.

Reading Comprehension

Answer the following questions.

1. Why is Surya considered the time-keeper of the world?
2. Why did Sanjana run away?
3. What was the name of the sun god in ancient Egypt?
4. How did Re make humans?
5. Who was the Japanese sun goddess?
6. How did the gods trick Amaterasu?

Vocabulary

Complete the following sentences by choosing words from the box.

pilot tailor doctor chef postman teacher cobbler waiter

A *pilot* flies airplanes.

A ____________________ serves food in a restaurant.

A ____________________ sews clothes.

A ____________________ delivers letters.

A ____________________ cooks food.

A ____________________ heals patients.

A ____________________ teaches children.

A ____________________ mends shoes.

Grammar

We add -ing to doing words (verbs) to indicate that the actions are happening right now.

Fill in the blanks by adding –ing to the word in brackets.

Mehak is *eating* a cake. (eat)

Amandeep is ____________________ in the lake. (swim)

We are ____________________ for an exam. (study)

She is always ___________________. (read)

The seniors are ___________________ football. (play)

Daddy is _________________ his shirt. (iron)

My sister is _____________________ a picture. (draw)

Fill in the blanks with has, have or had.

My grandparents ________________ a new house.

Khursheed _______________Malini's notebook.

Yesterday we ______________ ice cream for dessert.

We ________________ the cleanest classroom in the school.

Your father ______________ come home.

On my birthday I ________________ a big party.

Spelling and Punctuation

Read aloud the following words.

diet **pie** **lie** **drier** **client**

Now read these words.

chief **shield** **field** **cookie** **diesel**

How do you think these words are pronounced?

genie	flier	aunties	quiet
tries	vie	belief	piece

Writing

What did you do during your summer holidays? Describe in a few sentences.

You could use words like the ones given in the box.

journey travel heat play ice cream rest read

Listening

Listen carefully to the sentences that your teacher reads out and write them down.

Speaking

Have a conversation with your classmate. Ask questions about what each of you like to do. Use the phrases I like, I do not like and Do you like …?

Everyday English

When we want someone to do something for us, we say please.

- Please help me to do this sum.
- Please shut the door.
- Please give the newspaper.

Ask your partner to do the following things for you.

- Let you borrow an eraser.
- Stand in line.
- Sit down.
- Talk quietly.
- Help you to tie your shoelaces.

Activity

Colouring

Colour the sun, moon and stars in the picture below.

8 In the Desert

Ms Frizzle and her class take a trip on the Magic School Bus to see how animals live in the desert in The Magic School Bus Gets All Dried Up.

The sun in the desert was hot, hot, hot! We all started to sweat. Except for Ms Frizzle. She always keeps her cool. "Come along, class," she said. "We are here to experience the desert!"

Before long, we saw a hungry roadrunner chasing a lizard across the desert sand.

"Quick!" Phoebe exclaimed. "Everyone back on the bus! We have to save that lizard!"

Ms Frizzle's eyes lit up with an idea. Inside the bus, she pulled a lever. The bus started getting smaller. It turned into a lizard! And now the roadrunner was after us.

Ms Frizzle stepped hard on the gas pedal … and moved on!

A few seconds later, the roadrunner scooped us up in his beak! How could we get out of this? Arnold checked his trip manual.

roadrunner: a bird that runs swiftly
lever: a projecting handle used to operate a machine
scooped: picked up
manual: book which tells you how to do or use something

"To avoid being eaten, become something inedible," he read. "What does that mean?"

"It means we should become something that cannot be eaten," Dorothy Ann explained.

Ms Frizzle pulled another lever. The bus shook crazily, and then turned into a spiky horned lizard! The roadrunner spat us out. It did not like lizards with spikes.

"So, the little animals here have special ways to avoid being eaten," Phoebe said, "like being prickly."

"Yes, that is right," said Ms. Frizzle.

Next, Phoebe wanted to help a desert tortoise. "How would you like to be a tortoise roasting in the hot desert sun?" she asked.

Ms Frizzle's eyes glimmered. "As I always say, there is more than one way to beat the heat," she said. "Everyone, back into the bus."

Whirrr! Spin! Shrink, shrink. The bus grew a tough shell. Then, it burrowed down, down, down, way under the ground.

"Ah, so this is what it is like to be a desert tortoise," said Ms Frizzle.

Then, everything went dark. "Where are we?" Tim shouted.

"In a tortoise burrow. An underground shelter," Ms Frizzle explained.

We kept cool in our turtle burrow until the sun went down. When we went back outside—wow! The desert was suddenly a very busy place. It was full of animals.

"What happened?" cried Keesha.

Arnold looked at his manual. "To beat the heat, do like most desert animals. Come out only at night."

---

glimmered: shone dimly
burrowed: dug in

Reading Comprehension

Answer the following questions.

1. What was chasing the lizard?
2. How did the class save the lizard?
3. How does a desert tortoise beat the heat?
4. Why do desert animals only come out at night?
5. A tortoise lives in a burrow. Which other animals live underground?

Vocabulary

Underline the odd word in the following sets.

plane	train	bus	house	car
frog	fish	turtle	shark	tiger
water	milk	sandwich	juice	lassi
Delhi	Europe	Bangalore	Chennai	Mumbai
lizard	koel	crow	parrot	peacock

There are many words that we can use to describe the weather.

Underline the words that describe the weather.

It was a rainy day, so we went out and jumped in the puddles.

When it is sunny and warm, we play cricket in the park.

It was windy, so mummy's newspaper was blown away.

We will stay inside because it is so cloudy.

It was a dark and stormy night.

Grammar

When we add -d or -ed to a doing word (verb), it shows that the action has already happened.

Complete the following sentences by adding -d or -ed to the words in brackets.

After school I _______________ my homework before going outside to play. (complete)

In class I _________________ all the questions. (answer)

Sheela ____________________ the plants in the garden. (water)

Before you were born your parents _________________ in that house. (live)

The dog _________________ at the big grey cat. (bark)

Amir __________________ to listen to music. (like)

The waiter _______________ chocolate cake to the customers. (serve)

Yasmin's cat __________________ to the top of the tree. (climb)

Underline the describing words (adjectives) in the following sentences. How many of them are numbers?

The moon was big, white and round.

The mother cat had five fluffy kittens.

In my bag I was carrying two water bottles and five small cups.

The children picked many golden mangoes from the tree.

After lunch the three children played in a big, green field.

Spelling and Punctuation

Question marks

Question marks (?) are used at the end of questions.

Kaushik has come to his friend Aswath's house to find out why Aswath didn't come to school today.

Read the conversation between the two boys and fill in the missing capital letters, full stops and question marks.

KAUSHIK: hello aswath!

ASWATH: hi kaushik!

KAUSHIK: why didn't you come to school today

ASWATH: I am not well I have a cold

KAUSHIK: get well soon

ASWATH: thanks who won the football match

KAUSHIK: class four

ASWATH: I will come back to school next week

KAUSHIK: okay take care

ASWATH: bye

KAUSHIK: bye

Read the following words. How are they pronounced?

knead	**kn**ob	**kn**ight	**kn**uckle
knock	**kn**ack	**kn**ow	

Can you identify these kn words? Use the pictures as clues.

kn _ _ _

kn _ _

kn _ _ _

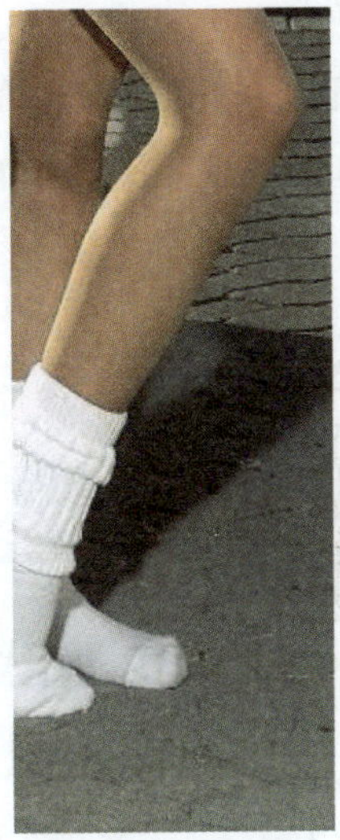

kn _ _

Writing

Frame questions for the statements given below.

____?

Yes, that is my elder sister.

____?

No, my father is a doctor, not a teacher.

____?

Yes, my new dress is blue and white.

____?

Yes, we are all travelling to Sri Lanka.

____?

No, that is not my house.

Listening

Your teacher will read a tongue-twister. Try to repeat it after him/her. See how fast you can repeat it.

Speaking

Take turns with your partner. One of you can make a simple statement and the other can give suggestions.

- I am going to watch television.
- Watch the cartoon channel.

You could use the following words:

thirsty/juice	tired/nap
buy flowers/roses	read a new book/this one

Activity

Desert objects

Tick the things you can find in a desert.

camel ☐	penguin ☐	palm tree ☐
sand ☐	dolphin ☐	pine tree ☐

The Owl and the Pussycat 9

This magical poem is by Edward Lear (1812-1888).

The Owl and the Pussycat went to sea
In a beautiful pea-green boat,
They took some honey, and plenty of money,
Wrapped up in a five-pound note.
The Owl looked up to the stars above,
And sang to a small guitar,
"O lovely Pussy! O Pussy my love,
What a beautiful Pussy you are,
You are, you are!
What a beautiful Pussy you are!"

Pussy said to the Owl, "You elegant fowl!
How charmingly sweet you sing!
O let us be married! Too long we have tarried:
But what shall we do for a ring?"
They sailed away, for a year and a day,

elegant: refined and tasteful
fowl: bird
tarried: delayed

To the land where the Bong-tree grows
And there in a wood a Piggy-wig stood
With a ring at the end of his nose,
His nose, his nose,
With a ring at the end of his nose.

"Dear Pig, are you willing to sell for one shilling
Your ring?" Said the Piggy, "I will."
So they took it away, and were married next day
By the Turkey who lives on the hill.
They dined on mince, and slices of quince,
Which they ate with a runcible spoon;
And hand in hand, on the edge of the sand,
They danced by the light of the moon,
The moon, the moon,
They danced by the light of the moon.

shilling: a unit of currency no longer in use
mince: meat chopped into small pieces
quince: a yellow fruit
runcible: a word created by Lear. Now means a fork with three short tines

Reading Comprehension

Answer the following questions.

1. How did the Owl and the Pussycat travel?
2. What did they take with them?
3. For how long did they sail?
4. Who sold them the ring?
5. What did the Owl and the Pussycat do at the end of the poem?

Vocabulary

The Pig had a ring on the end of his nose. How would you describe your body?

Choose words from the box that can be used to describe the different parts of your body.

You can use the same word more than once, if you like.

long big short small red brown black white wide curly straight bright shiny soft pink blue round thin

eyes ____

ears ____

nose ____

cheeks ____

mouth ______________________________

neck ______________________________

hair ______________________________

Listening

Listen to the sentences your teacher reads out and count the number of describing words.

Speaking

Ask your partner questions based on the words in the box.

summer winter holidays family home pets ice cream

- What did you do in the summer?
- I ate lots of ice cream.

Activity

Nursery rhymes

Draw a line to connect the parts of the nursery rhymes.

Jack and Jill	runs through the town
Wee Willie Winkie	sat on a wall
Humpty Dumpty	has lost her sheep
Little Bo Peep	went up the hill

10 Helen Keller

This is the story of a woman who was deaf and dumb, but managed to live an inspiring life. This piece is taken from The Best Days of My Life *by Scharada Dubey.*

The well stood in the garden at a small distance from the main house. The deaf and blind girl walked along the path to the well, holding her teacher Anne Sullivan's hand. When they reached, the teacher drew her pupil's hand and put it under the water spout, letting the cool stream of the water flow over the girl's hand.

Then gently holding the girl's other hand, the teacher pressed her finger into the child's palm and spelt the word "water". This simple act opened a whole new world for her intelligent student. This little girl, who

spout: where water comes out

was so severely handicapped that she could not understand speech and language, learnt thirty new words that same afternoon. The teacher and her pupil had found a way to overcome Helen's handicaps and communicate.

This afternoon of April 5, 1887, was the beginning of Helen's triumph over disability that would bring hope for millions of people in the future. From then on, Helen made great progress, and her ability to learn was truly amazing, considering her double handicap. Anne first taught Helen to read with raised letters, then with Braille, and to write with both ordinary and Braille typewriters.

After finishing her education, Helen became an activist and spoke out against child labour. She wrote many books and articles on blindness, deafness, social issues and women's rights. Her most popular book is *The Story of My Life*. She met many famous people, who admired her courage, and received many honours, including the United States' Presidential Medal of Freedom.

triumph: victory
Braille: a system of writing or printing for use by the blind
activist: someone who works for a cause

Reading Comprehension

Answer the following questions.

1. How did Anne Sullivan teach Helen new words?
2. How did Helen read and write?
3. What did Helen do after completing her education?

Vocabulary

Fill in the opposites of the given words.

happy	______________	win	______________
shallow	______________	frown	______________
cold	______________	buy	______________
thick	______________	come	______________
clever	______________	disappear	______________

Grammar

Nouns and verbs

Underline the naming words and circle the doing words. Then write them in the given table.

Lakshmi is watering the plants.

The monkey has climbed up the tree.

Your brother is learning to drive a car.

Karan fell off his bicycle.

Harjeet works very hard.

We cannot cook food.

I want to read a new book.

Sophie gave the teacher an apple.

Naming Words	Doing Words

Spelling and Punctuation

Read aloud the following words ending in -ss.

grass pass press boss loss toss

class dress confess guess less

Read aloud the following words ending in -sh.

push bush brush lush hush wash

ash mash lash fresh flesh

Writing

The following statements make a story. But they are in the wrong order!

Number them in the correct order to tell the story.

There were no other children in the palace for him to play with. ☐

The voice said, "Excuse me, can you help me to find my ball?" ☐

Once upon a time there lived a prince. ☐

"Of course I will help you!" said the prince. ☐

And from that day the prince and the dog were best friends. ☐

Then one day while sitting in the garden he heard a voice. ☐

The prince was very lonely. ☐

The prince looked around and saw a big dog. He was surprised. ☐

So the prince and the dog looked for the ball, and when they found it they played for hours. ☐

Listening

Your teacher will call out instructions. Listen carefully and act them out.

Speaking

Which are your favourite subjects? Which subjects are hard or boring? Discuss with the class.

Activity

Make a bookworm

How do you keep track of all the books you have read so far?
Use this bookworm to keep your book records.

You will need:

- Coloured chart paper in various colours • Scissors • Markers

Method:

1. Draw circles of radius 2" on the chart paper. Draw at least ten circles.
2. Cut them out neatly.

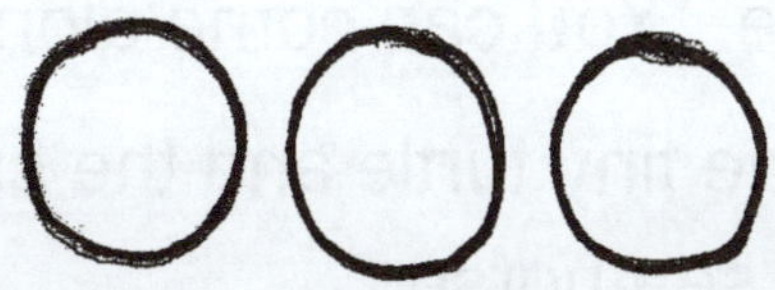

3. On one circle, draw or stick a pair of eyes and a smiley mouth. This will be the bookworm's face. Make little antennae for the head.

4. Stick the face on the wall in your room.
5. As you finish reading a book, write the name of the book, the author and the date you finished reading it on a circle.
6. Attach this circle to the head of the bookworm.
7. Keep adding circles as you finish more and more books.
8. Your bookworm will keep on growing and so will your reading skills.

11 Tiny Turtle Wants a Friend

In this story you will meet many creatures who live in the sea.

The tiny turtle is very lonely. He looks under a rock and sees a crazy crab.

"I want to find a friend," says the tiny turtle.

"I can be your friend," says the crab.

"I am looking for a small turtle like me," says the tiny turtle. "You can come along if you like."

The tiny turtle and the crazy crab look behind a bottle and see a silly sea horse.

"I want to find a friend," says the tiny turtle.

"I can be your friend," says the sea horse.

"I am looking for a small turtle like me," says the tiny turtle. "You can come along if you like."

The tiny turtle, the crazy crab and the silly sea horse look among some brown seaweed and see a shy shrimp.

"I want to find a friend," says the tiny turtle.

"I can be your friend," says the shrimp.

"I am looking for a small turtle like me," says the tiny turtle. "You can come along if you like."

The tiny turtle, the crazy crab, the silly sea horse and the shy shrimp look inside a cave and see a jolly jellyfish.

"I want to find a friend," say the tiny turtle.

"I can be your friend," says the jellyfish.

"I am looking for a turtle," says the tiny turtle. "You can come along if you like."

The tiny turtle, the crazy crab, the silly sea horse, the shy shrimp and the jolly jellyfish look on the sandy seafloor and see a talkative old turtle.

"I want to find a friend," says the tiny turtle. "I am looking for a small turtle like me."

"Your friends are not those who look like you, but those who stay with you," says the old turtle wisely. "You seem to have a lot of friends already!"

The tiny turtle looked around, and saw that the talkative old turtle was right!

"I don't need to find a small turtle like me!" says the tiny turtle. "I have so many wonderful friends already!"

Reading Comprehension

Answer the following questions.

1. What was the tiny turtle looking for?
2. What sort of friend did the tiny turtle want?
3. Where did the tiny turtle and the crazy crab find the sea horse?
4. Who did they find inside a cave?
5. Write the names of all the sea animals that you come across in the story.

Vocabulary

What sounds do these animals make? Match the animal to the sound.

Animal	Sound
dog	roar
duck	moo
cat	grunt
pig	quack
owl	meow
lion	bark
frog	hoot
cow	cluck
hen	croak

Grammar

Making a sentence

Put the words in the correct order to make a short sentence.

Don't forget to start the first word with a capital letter and end the sentence with a full stop.

1. my this is house
2. sing likes Selina to
3. ball that yellow is
4. draw we pictures crayons with
5. mother tall your is very
6. has a he new bag

Tick the sentences below.

My name is Malavika.	☐
the door	☐
That chair is broken.	☐
You are very late.	☐
the purple dress	☐

Words that help

Some words help the **doing words** (verbs). These words, called the **helping verbs**, are used along with other doing words in a sentence. Helping verbs have no meaning on their own. They help the main verb (which has the real meaning). Examples of helping verbs are is, am, are, was and were.

Complete the following sentences using is, am, are, was or were.

She ______ very busy.

Yesterday I ________ not well.

My friends ________ in Dehradun.

Chiragh's sisters ___________ born in Indore.

Last year Rahul ________ the best student.

I ________ going to watch a movie.

Spelling and Punctuation

Read aloud the following words.

eat	bean	sea	wheat	meat
pea	beak	heat	leaf	

Read aloud the following words.

rear clear idea fear ear

Can you notice a difference in the way ea is pronounced? Now read out these words.

sweat death deaf wear

How many ea words can you think of? How are they pronounced?

Writing

Look carefully at the picture. Make a short story about what you see in it.

Listening

Your teacher will read out some sentences. Listen carefully and count the number of doing words that you hear.

Speaking

Talk to your partner about your best friend.

Some of the phrases you might use are:

- My friend's name is _______.
- He/She is ______ years old.

Use describing words such as tall, short, kind, clever, funny, nice and sweet.

Activity

Pet puzzler

Tania's parents gave her a pet for her birthday. Can you tell which pet they gave her.

- It doesn't have fur.
- It doesn't eat meat.
- It cannot fly.

Colour Tania's pet.

Four Little Tigers 12

Tigers are in danger. They are being hunted for many reasons. This poem is funny, but it also has a serious message!

Four little tigers
Sitting in a tree;
One became a lady's coat,
Now there's only three.

Three little tigers
Under a sky of blue;
One became a rich man's rug,
Now there's only two.

Two little tigers
Sleeping in the sun;
One a hunter's trophy made,
Now there's only one.

One little tiger
Waiting to be had;
OOOPS, he got the hunter first,
Aren't you kind of glad?

Reading Comprehension

Answer the following questions.

1. How many tigers were there in the beginning?
2. What happened to the second tiger?
3. What happened to the hunter?
4. How many tigers were there at the end?
5. Do human beings treat tigers and other wild animals well?

Vocabulary

Match the pairs of rhyming words.

eight	two
do	egg
six	late
leg	mix

Tigers are endangered because so many of them have been hunted. Other animals are also endangered.

Can you name these endangered animals?

What do you find in your kitchen? Make a list of all the objects you can remember.

Unscramble the letters to name the objects.

DGFIRE	OTTARSE	NOPOS	VONE
OTSEV	NEUPASAC	TELPA	LOBW

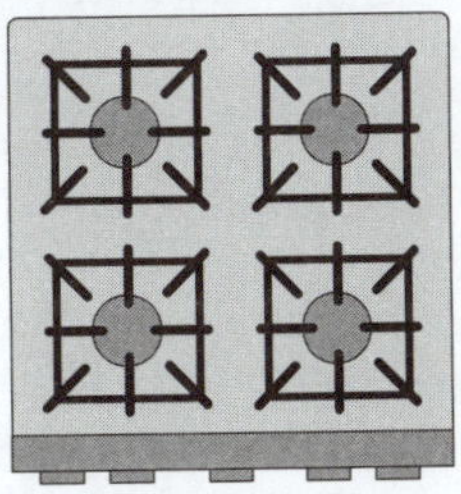  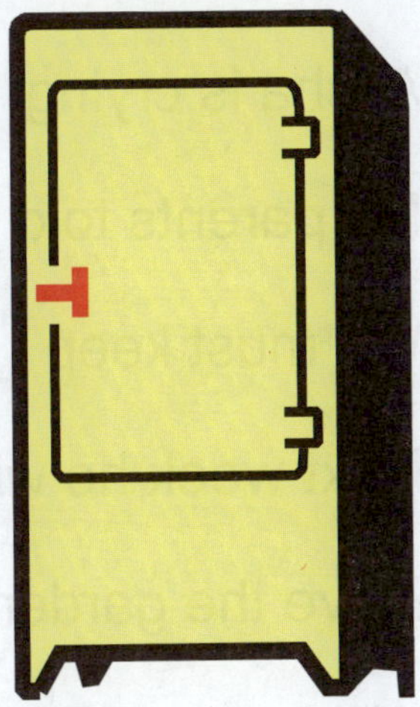

 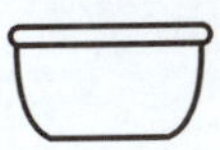 

Grammar

Pronouns

Pronouns are words that take the place of a noun. We can use a pronoun instead of a noun.

When referring to a person or people we often use the words I, me, you, your, he, his, she, her, they, their, we, us, our, it and its. For example, instead of saying Mihir is my friend. This is Mihir's house, we can say Mihir is my friend. This is his house.

Fill in the blanks using the pronouns given above.

Your grandparents have sold _______ house.

My parents and I went on a holiday. ________ went to Darjeeling.

Alisha is crying. ________ has lost _________ pen.

My parents told _______ to finish the work.

We must keep _______ classroom clean.

Next week he will visit ______ family. ________ live in Jamshedpur.

I love the garden. ______ is a very pretty place.

Will ______ come to _______ house for dinner tomorrow?

All _________ friends will come for the school play.

You look very nice in ___________ new clothes.

Complete the following sentences using this, that, these or those.

__________ boys are behaving very badly.

__________ flower is prettier than ___________ one.

I made ___________ cookies for you.

____________ girl is going to win the race.

___________ book is very exciting.

Spelling and Punctuation

Read aloud the following words.

clap	**clip**	**cloth**	**clock**	**cleft**
cling	**cliff**	**clay**	**class**	**flock**
floss	**flap**	**flush**	**flip**	**flick**
flare	**fly**	**place**	**plate**	**plump**
pluck	**play**	**plan**	**plait**	**plank**

Rewrite the following sentences with correct punctuation marks.

1. where is my book
2. anshuman took it home last night
3. why hasn't he come to school today
4. he is unwell
5. his sister sarika is also unwell
6. i will go to their house after school
7. who would like to come with me
8. we will all come with you, manav

Writing

Write five sentences about tigers. You may also draw a picture in the space provided.

Listening

Your teacher will read out some tiger facts. Say whether they are true or false.

Speaking

Pretend that you and your partner are cooking together in a kitchen. Have a conversation.

The phrases in the box will help you.

May I have ________? Can you pass me the ________ please?
Thank you

Yes, of course   You're welcome   Here it is   Where is the______?

Everyday English

When asking for permission we use the phrase may I ...?

Ask your teacher for permission to do the following:

- Stand up
- Sit down
- Go and drink water
- Play a game
- Go home

13 Sir No-name

What happens if you are a princess, and the only sister in a family of four children? Find out in this extract from The Princess Knight *by the internationally bestselling author Cornelia Funke.*

King Wilfred had three sons. They were taught all the things he had been taught as a child. They learned riding, fighting with swords and good table manners too. They even learned jousting, a contest with a spear on horseback.

The king also had a baby daughter called Violetta. He decided to teach her the same lessons that he had taught his sons. But she was so small that she couldn't even lift a sword!

Her brothers teased her. "Itsy-Bitsy Little Vi—little girl can't hurt a fly!" They would show off about how strong they were, and laugh at their little sister as she struggled to mount a horse.

"Oh, Emma," said Violetta to her nursemaid, "I'll never be as strong as my brothers."

"Not as strong, maybe, but you are three times as clever," said Emma sensibly.

Violetta started slipping out of the castle secretly and practising all the things her brothers could do. Slowly, she got better at fighting and riding. Violetta became so quick that when her brothers practised jousting with her, their spears just hit empty air. Soon, they stopped laughing at her.

One day, the king called her and said, "There is a jousting tournament tomorrow. All the bravest knights will come to the castle. The prize will be your hand in marriage."

Violetta was so upset on hearing this that she ran out of the room in tears.

"Stop crying, sister!" said Violetta's brother. "I'll make sure I win the tournament. You certainly can't marry me!"

"Thank you," said Violetta, "but I think I'd better just see to it myself."

The next day, hundreds of knights came to fight in the tournament. King Wilfred sat down to watch. Violetta put on her helmet and blackest armour and rode into the field with the other knights. She gave her name as Sir No-name.

The tournament began. Knight after knight rode into the arena but Sir No-name defeated them all. By the end, there was no one left who was willing to fight. And Sir No-name rode over to the king to receive the prize.

"You shall marry my daughter," said the king.

"Oh, I don't think so!" Sir No-name replied, raising his helmet.

"Hello, Father," said Violetta. "What is the prize for a Princess Knight?"

Reading Comprehension

Answer the following questions.

1. How many children did King Wilfred have?
2. Who was Emma?
3. Why did Violetta slip out of the castle at night?
4. What was the prize for the jousting tournament?
5. Who was Sir no-Name?

Vocabulary

Violetta travelled on a horse. How many different transport vehicles can you name? How many have you travelled in?

Look at the pictures and name the vehicles.

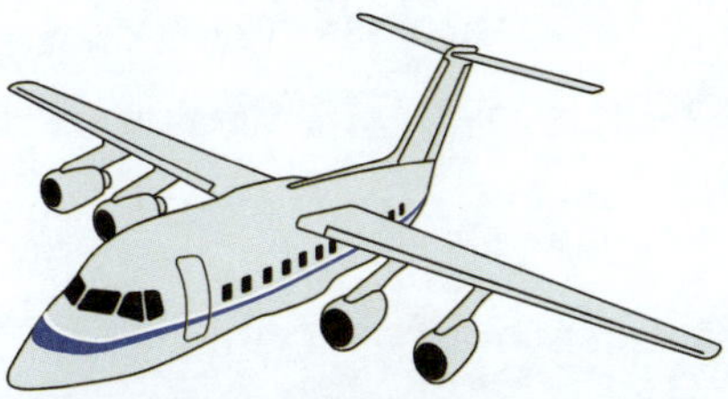

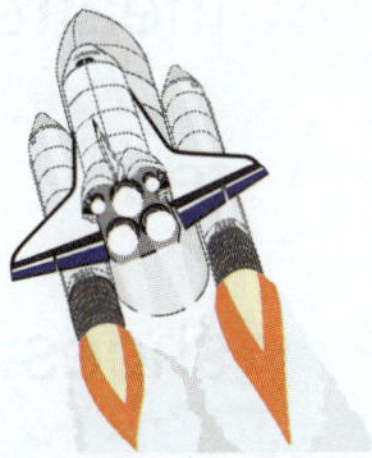

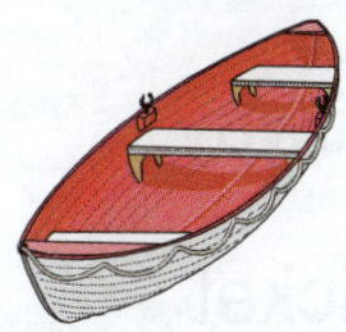

How many vehicle names can you find in this grid?

P	O	B	O	A	T	K	C	M
B	R	I	C	K	S	H	A	W
U	S	C	T	A	N	K	R	A
S	H	Y	K	T	A	X	I	T
R	O	C	K	E	T	E	T	G
A	S	L	T	R	A	I	N	Y
A	H	E	H	T	R	U	C	K
D	I	S	P	L	A	N	E	C
S	P	A	C	E	S	H	I	P

Some pairs of words are often used together.

Match the following sets of words.

dancing	court
hot	ice cream
tennis	bat
cup	theatre
railway	tea
cricket	shoes
movie	saucer
chocolate	station

Grammar

Fill in the blanks using **there is**, **there are**, **there was** or **there were**.

Last week ________________________ five goldfish in the pond.

Now ______________________ only one.

_____________________ five games periods during the school week.

Yesterday _________________________ a lot of traffic.

________________________ a guard on duty at the school gate.

Question words

When we ask questions, we use the words **why**, **when**, **how** and **where**.

Put a tick against the questions and a cross against the sentences.

Where is your pencil box? ☐

My sharpener is missing. ☐

How was your exam? ☐

When are you coming home? ☐

Shikha has made dinner. ☐

The doctor is very busy. ☐

Why did you shout at her? ☐

How do you tie your shoelaces? ☐

Spelling and Punctuation

Read aloud the following words.

doct**or**	mirr**or**	act**or**	edit**or**	auth**or**
counsell**or**	anch**or**	camph**or**	panth**er**	amb**er**
ang**er**	rid**er**	answ**er**	hung**er**	fing**er**

Writing

Violetta lived in a castle. Where do you live?

Describe your home in a few short sentences.

Use some of the words in the box.

cosy	big	small	house	flat	bedroom	happy

Listening

Your teacher will read out the names of some things that are associated with a particular colour. Listen carefully and call out the name of the colour.

Speaking

Violetta liked to fight with swords. What do you like to do?

Discuss your hobbies with your partner using short sentences.

Use phrases like I like to, I enjoy, I am good at.

Activity

Crossword

Can you complete this crossword with the names of people and things you might meet in a book?

ACROSS

3 large creature who breathes fire

4 daughter of queen

5 a man who fights

DOWN

1 small woman with wings and a wand

2 a creature like a horse, but with one single horn

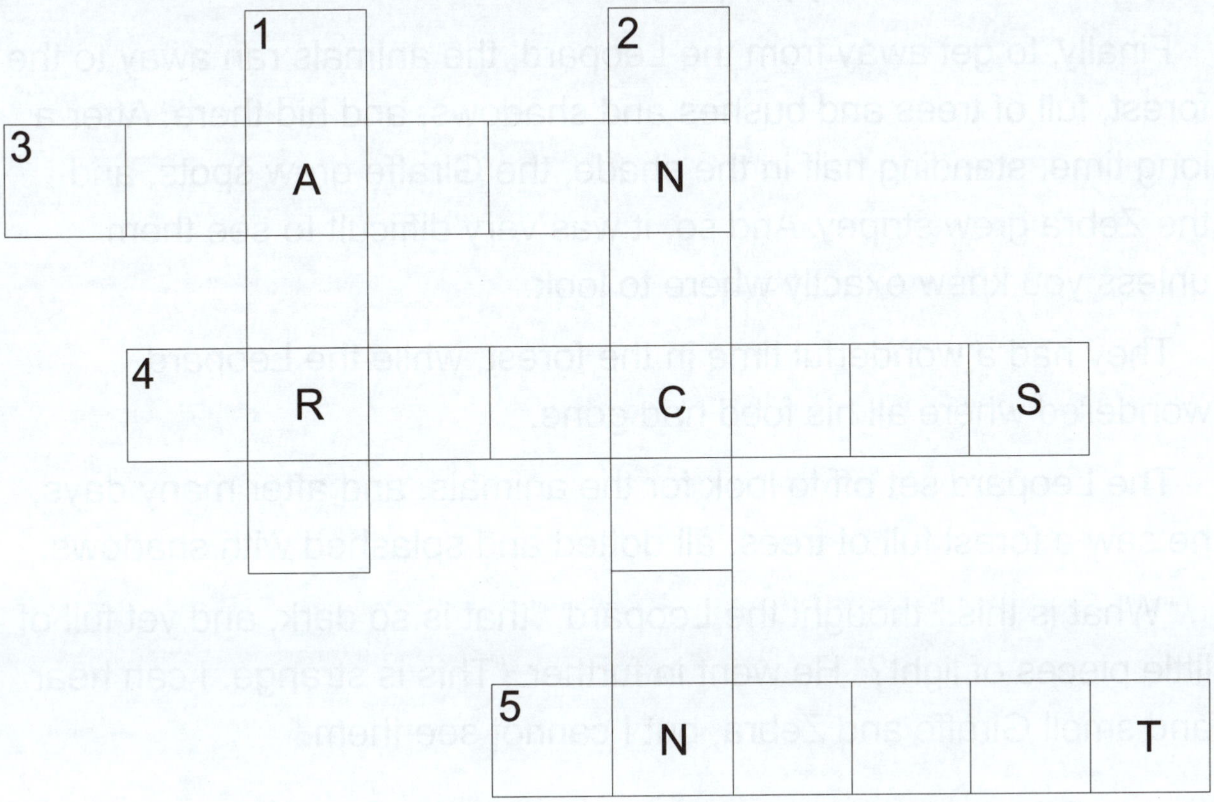

14 How the Leopard Got its Spots

This story is taken from Just So Stories *by Rudyard Kipling.*

Many years ago, the Leopard lived in a place which was hot, with sand and sandy-yellowish stones and grass. The Giraffe and the Zebra lived there; and they were sandy-yellow-brownish all over. But the Leopard was the sandiest-yellowish-brownest of them all.

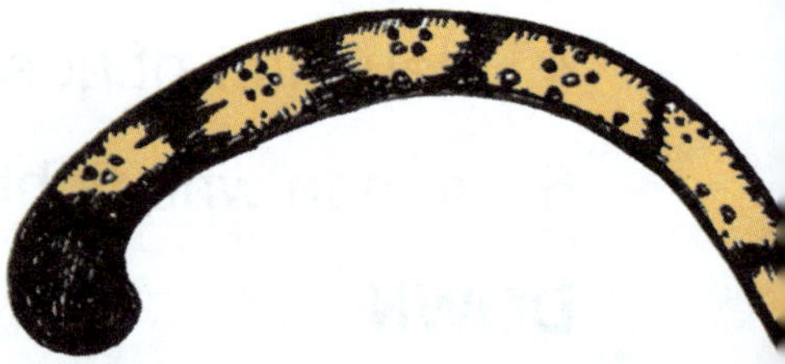

This was very bad for the Giraffe and Zebra; for the Leopard would lie down by the yellowish-brownish stones or grass, and surprise the animals by jumping out at them.

Finally, to get away from the Leopard, the animals ran away to the forest, full of trees and bushes and shadows, and hid there. After a long time, standing half in the shade, the Giraffe grew spots, and the Zebra grew stripey. And so, it was very difficult to see them unless you knew exactly where to look.

They had a wonderful time in the forest, while the Leopard wondered where all his food had gone.

The Leopard set off to look for the animals, and after many days, he saw a forest full of trees, all dotted and splashed with shadows.

"What is this," thought the Leopard, "that is so dark, and yet full of little pieces of light?" He went in further. "This is strange. I can hear and smell Giraffe and Zebra, but I cannot see them."

The Leopard hunted all day but he never saw them. That night, he heard the Zebra and Giraffe, so he knocked them down and said, "I am going to sit on you till morning so that I can see you."

In the morning, the Leopard said, "What is this? The Giraffe has chestnut spots and the Zebra has black stripes. How did you do this?"

"Like this," said the Zebra and moved to some bushes where the sunlight fell all stripey, and Giraffe moved to some tallish trees where the shadows fell in patches.

All the Leopard could see were stripey and spotted shadows. The Zebra and Giraffe had hidden themselves in the shadowy forest.

"That is a trick worth learning," said the Leopard. "I need to match my background."

So he told a man passing by, "If you want to live, make some spots on my skin." The man dipped his five fingers in black paint, put his fingertips close together and pressed them all over the Leopard, and wherever the five fingers touched they left five little black marks. If you look closely at any Leopard now, you will see that there are always five spots—of five black fingertips.

Reading Comprehension

Answer the following questions.

1. Where did the Leopard live?
2. What colour were the Giraffe, Zebra and Leopard?
3. What happened to the Giraffe and Zebra in the forest?
4. Who told Leopard where the other animals were?
5. Why does a Leopard have spots?

Vocabulary

Sometimes, two different words can have almost the same meaning.

Match the following sets of words with similar meanings.

jungle	cookie
beautiful	scared
sad	forest
meadow	quick
huge	chat
fast	unhappy
talk	pupil
frightened	big
biscuit	field
student	pretty

Write the names of the items of clothing.

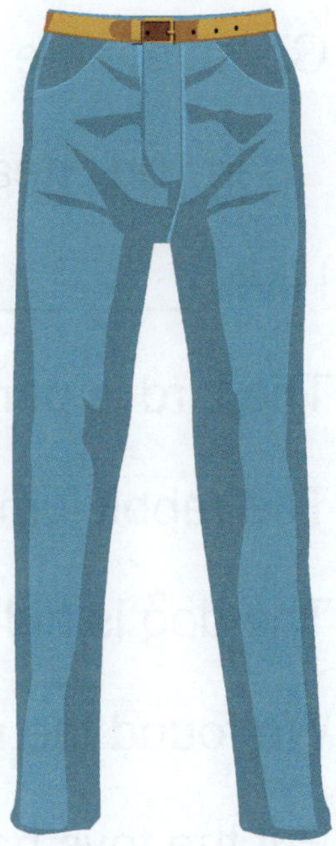

Which of these clothes are you wearing at the moment?

We wear different clothes for different occasions. What would you wear for the following?

sports day | a religious function | sleeping
a party | school

Grammar

Prepositions

Prepositions are words we use to show the relationship of a noun or a pronoun to another word in the sentence. They can be called place words because they often tell us the position of things.

Complete the following sentences using the prepositions in the box.

in on near over under up down into with beside above

I live _______________ the bus stop.

The bird is perched ___________ the branch.

The rabbit jumped _____________ the stream.

The dog is hiding ________________ the bed.

We found the missing book ___________ the cupboard.

Put the toys back ______________ their boxes.

We got into the elevator and went __________ to the tenth floor.

The papers are on the shelf ____________ the table.

There is a hut ______________ by the river.

Put your tie _____________ the drawer ___________ your socks.

Spelling and Punctuation

Read aloud the following words.

li**ck**	che**ck**	si**ck**	thi**ck**	mo**ck**
flo**ck**	ba**ck**	ne**ck**	clu**ck**	sa**ck**
sweet	**sw**im	**sw**ing	**sw**at	**sw**allow
swap	**sw**amp	**sw**ell	**sw**ift	**sw**ay

Writing

Look at the picture below. Describe it in short sentences.

The words in the box may help you.

big grey wise strong tusks forests India Africa trunk ears

Listening

Your teacher will read sets of three words. Two of the words will have the same meaning. Find the odd one out.

Speaking

Have a conversation with your partner about what foods you like and which you don't.

- Do you like milk?
- No, I do not like milk.
- Do you like cakes?
- Yes, I love cakes.

Use some of the suggestions in the box.

cheese carrots spinach beans rice chocolate

Activity

Colouring

Colour the pictures of the leopard, the zebra and the giraffe in the correct colours and patterns based on what you have learnt from the story.

15 *I'm a Real Boy!*

What does it mean to be a boy? Find out in this poem by Clayton Koh.

I'm a real boy
When I'm leading the team.
When we score a goal
I cheer and I scream!

I'm a real boy
When I'm last to be picked.
I'll still try my best
When it's my chance to kick.

I'm a real boy
When I look like the rest.
You can't pick me out
By the way that I'm dressed.

I'm a real boy
When I'm bold and unique.
I can choose to wear pink
And not be a geek!

I'm a real boy
When I'm stoic and strong
When they call me sissy
Like I don't belong.

I'm a real boy
When their words make me sad,
This time I cry,
I'm feeling so bad.

I'm a real boy
When I play with the boys.
We play the same games.
We like the same toys.

I'm a real boy
When the girls and I play.
They're quite fun to talk to.
They have lots to say.

Reading Comprehension

Mark true (T) or false (F).

The poet is not a real boy if he wears pink. [ ]

The poet is a real boy when he cries. [ ]

Real boys cannot play with girls. [ ]

The poet is a real boy because of the clothes he wears. [ ]

The poet is willing to be himself. [ ]

Vocabulary

Complete the following comparisons using words from the box. Add a, an or the where necessary.

pie   snail   daisy   lamb   toast   ox   fox   lion

As fresh as ____________   As strong as ____________

As gentle as ____________   As easy as ____________

As brave as ____________   As warm as ____________

As slow as ____________   As cunning as ____________

Grammar

Joining words

When we want to join two short sentences to make a longer sentence, we use words like and and but.

The cat is black. The dog is white.

The cat is black **but** the dog is white.

Rishi is clever. Rishi is funny.

Rishi is clever **and** funny.

Use and or but to join the following sets of sentences.

1. My garden is small. My garden is beautiful.
2. Ma likes to drink coffee. Papa likes to drink tea.
3. Sukhmani plays the piano. Sukhmani plays the violin.
4. Apples are sweet. Lemons are sour.
5. My brother is tall. My sister is tall.
6. Mallika likes blue. Mallika likes yellow.
7. Gopal is eating a sandwich. Gopal is eating a biscuit.
8. Anant likes to read books. Deepak does not like to read books.

Underline the nouns in **red**, the verbs in **yellow**, the adjectives in **blue**, the pronouns in **green**, and the prepositions in **purple**.

My red hat is on the table.

The train has arrived very early.

Indra is waiting for her mother.

I am going to buy some fresh fruits from the market.

Please put on your coat before you go out.

Put the new clothes into the cupboard.

Spelling and Punctuation

Read aloud the following words.

brave	brag	break	bright	brunt
drag	draft	drive	dread	dress
free	frame	fry	friend	front
try	trap	tramp	trail	troop

Complete the following words using the clues given in the brackets.

BR __ __ __ (we build houses with it)

FR __ __ __ (something that girls sometimes wear)

TR __ __ (a journey)

DR __ __ __ (where waste water goes)

TR __ __ __ (a mode of transport)

BR __ __ (sound made by a donkey)

DR __ __ __ (what we do when we're thirsty)

FR __ __ (an animal that lives in ponds)

Listening

Your teacher will read sentences with homonyms—two words which sound the same but have different meanings. Identify the homonyms in each sentence.

How are the two words spelt?

Speaking

What do you think boys like to do? What do you think girls like to do? Discuss with your class.

Everyday English

When we have done something wrong or are causing trouble to someone, we apologise. Some ways of apologising are:

I'm sorry   Excuse me   I beg your pardon.

What would you say if you did the following?

- bumped into someone in the corridor?
- broke your partner's pencil?
- were asking for directions?

Activity

Same or different?

Circle the two pictures in each box that are the same.

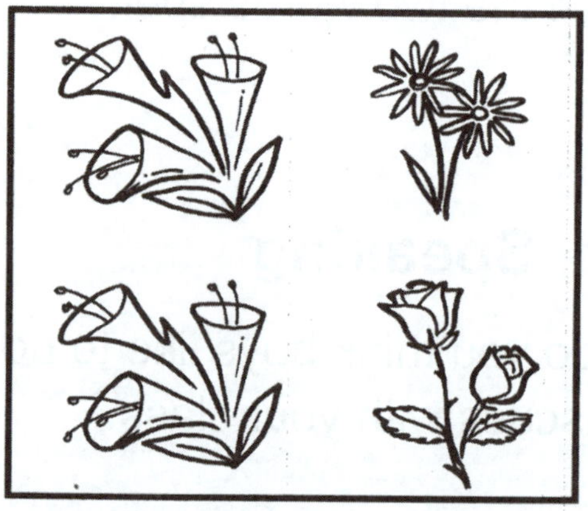

Listening texts

Lesson 2

This is my sister. Her name is Ishita. She studies in college. She has a cat named Joseph. She has long brown hair. She likes to listen to music and play the piano. She is my best friend. I love my sister.

Lesson 3

1. He is very big and strong. His wife is called a cow and his baby is called a calf.
2. She gives us wool. She eats grass.
3. She gives us milk. Her baby is a calf.
4. She likes to swim. She lays eggs. Her babies are called ducklings.

Lesson 5

1. A green triangle
2. A red circle
3. A blue square
4. A purple rectangle
5. An orange flower

Lesson 7

We are playing in the garden with our dog Spot. We throw a ball and Spot catches it. Spot runs around the garden. He is very funny to watch. We all laugh.

Lesson 8

Give papa a cup of proper coffee in a copper coffee cup.

Lesson 9

1. The clever crow picked up the small stones with his sharp beak.
2. Arun's mother gave him a plate of delicious food.
3. Early in the morning my mother drinks a big cup of hot coffee.
4. I have one green t-shirt and two red ones.

Lesson 10

Comb your hair.
Put on your tie.
Drink a glass of milk.
Wave goodbye.
Go to sleep.

Lesson 11

1. Amrita is eating cherries.
2. Sam is playing a game.
3. We are all enjoying the party.
4. Annie is drinking milk.
5. Amit wants a pet.

Lesson 12

1. Tigers are the largest cats.
2. Tigers have five legs.
3. Tigers are spotted.
4. Tigers are striped.
5. Tigers are vegetarian.

Lesson 13

1. Grass, leaves, jealousy
2. The sea, jeans, the sky, the Indian cricket team
3. Cherries, heat, roses, blood
4. Butter, the sun, bananas
5. Crown, medal, trophy

Lesson 14

1. Chair, seat, table
2. Eraser, rubber, sharpener
3. Pillow, cushion, curtain
4. Letter, note, postman
5. Forest, jungle, monkey

Lesson 15

1. The two boys had eaten too many chocolates.
2. Where is the t-shirt I wanted to wear?
3. Our friends will come here in an hour.
4. Riddhi ate eight sandwiches.
5. I don't know why there is no milk.

Evaluation Table

Name: ______________________
Class: ____________

Title	Comprehension		Vocabulary	Spelling and Punctuation	Grammar
	Reading for facts	Making inferences			
1. Jay and the Baby					
2. His Majesty's Moustache					
3. Springtime on the Farm					
4. A Dinosaur Was at My Door					
5. The Emperor and the Nightingale					
6. Eyes to See					
7. The Sun God					
8. In the Desert					
9. The Owl and the Pussycat					
10. Helen Keller					
11. Tiny Turtle Wants a Friend					
12. Four Little Tigers					
13. Sir No-name					
14. How the Leopard Got its Spots					
15. I'm a Real Boy!					

Writing			Speaking		Listening
Organisation of ideas	Making connections	Expression	Confdence	Fluency	

Acknowledgements

The publishers would like to thank the following for permission to use copyrighted material:

A. Edathatta and S. Onteddu for the illustrations for 'Eyes to See'; Anitha Bennet for the activity Make a Bookworm from *Papercraft* (Scholastic India: 2006) and the accompanying illustrations; Anupa Lal for 'His Majesty's Moustache' from *Birbal the Clever Courtier* (Scholastic India: 2007); Blake Education for the activities Little Words from Big Words, Nursery Rhymes, and Pet Puzzler and Same or Different? from *Brainteasers, Puzzles and Games* (Scholastic India: 2008); Clayton Koh for the text and illustrations of 'I'm a Real Boy' from *I'm a Real Boy* (Scholastic India: 2008); Malavika P.C. for the illustrations of 'Five Little Tigers' and the activity Join the Dots; Priya Kuriyan for the illustration for 'Springtime on the Farm' and the illustrations on p.19 and p.73; Priyankar Gupta for the illustrations for 'The Emperor and the Nightingale'; Scharada Dubey for 'Helen Keller' from *The Best Days of My Life* (Scholastic India: 2008); Scholastic Inc. for 'Springtime at the Farm' from *Just Right Plays: Twenty-five Emergent Reader Plays Around the Year* by Carol Pugliano-Martin (Scholastic Inc: 1999); 'In the Desert' from *The Magic School Bus Gets All Dried Up* (Scholastic Inc: 1996) and the accompanying illustrations by Bruce Degen; 'Eyes to See' and 'A Dinosaur Was At My Door' from *101 Thematic Poems* by Mary Sullivan (Scholastic Inc: 1999) and the accompanying illustrations for 'A Dinosaur Was At My Door'; Sheila Dhir for the text and illustrations for 'The Sun God' from *The Cowherd Prince and Other Gods and Goddesses* (Scholastic India: 2006); Shilpa Ranade for the illustration for 'His Majesty's Moustache', 'Tiny Turtle Wants a Friend' and 'How the Leopard Got its Spots'; Sumathi Sudhakar for 'Jay and the Baby' and the activity Safe or Unsafe? from *There's A New Baby at Home* (Scholastic India: 2006); Sunandini Basu for the illustrations for 'Jay and the Baby'; The Chicken House for 'Sir No-name' from *The Princess Knight* by Cornelia Funke (Chicken House: 2001) and the accompanying illustrations by Kerstin Meyer; Zainab Tambawallah for the illustration for 'Hellen Keller'.

While every attempt has been made to trace copyright holders for the text, illustrations and photographs, this has not been possible in all cases. Any omissions brought to our attention will be rectified in future editions.